THE ROAD TO HELL VIA THE A194

Best Wishes

Daryn Dodge

DARYN DODGE

The Road to hell, via the A194

ISBN 978-1-912009-92-3

Published by Compass-Publishing in 2017
www.compass-publishing.com

Printed in the United Kingdom by CPI Group UK Ltd (Croydon, CR0 4YY)

Edited and Typeset by Wrate's Editing Services, London
www.wrateseditingservices.co.uk

This book is dedicated to my father, Robert Edward Dodge, who sadly passed away just before it was completed.

He was a very special man who will always be in my heart, and to whom I will always be grateful.

Contents

Introduction

What the Heck?

It all seemed so completely ridiculous.

After all, I was supposed to be a mature, practical middle-aged man. But instead of being the sensible person I had come to know and love, I was being the exact opposite.

Here I was, determined to commit an act of surreal suicide, in the middle of 50,000 people, under the gaze of the majority of the North East's population *and* live TV cameras. It's one way of getting your 15-minutes of fame I guess, but it was definitely not what I'd had in mind.

This old, overweight, unfit body could only be pushed so far before it would decide to make the ultimate objection. That tipping point was looking closer with every step I ran.

I kept asking myself how I had managed to let myself get into this perilous situation. Unsurprisingly, it had involved a large amount of poor decision-making, commitments that I had little chance of delivering on and, in the most part, a huge amount of ego that just wasn't prepared to lose face and admit what we all really knew.

I thought back to how it had all started, two years earlier.

In the Beginning...

I'm afraid that unlike a certain Mr Forrest Gump, I do not subscribe to the theory that life is like a box of chocolates. At no point have the experiences of my life resembled the contents of a Quality Street tin.

Well, apart from the chocs that appear really promising, only to have a sickly centre that leaves a nasty taste in your mouth. And then there are the ones that seem a good idea, but turn out to be so tough it would be easier to chew a granite floor tile. But all is not lost, I guess. Amid all the unpleasant disappointments in life, there is always the Green Triangle and Vanilla Fudge.

When I look back, there have been a number of times in my life when I have used the phrase, "I didn't see that coming." However, on this occasion, I really didn't see any of this journey coming. If you had told me at the outset what was ahead of me, I would have said you were completely off your trolley, and that you'd have had more chance of spotting a dodo riding a unicorn. As bizarre as it will sound, everything in this book really did happen.

I have told my story a number of times at organised talks for various charity events. It's only natural that I would eventually feel the need to put it down on paper. And that point has arrived.

My story begins in February 2007. At that time I was a 46-year-old man living in Suffolk. I had three daughters and one granddaughter and, after divorcing five years earlier, lived on my own. And before you get carried away, I was not your stereotypical middle-aged bachelor, although others – and you, the reader – may disagree.

Now, what I do need to tell you is that I ran (and still run) my own management consultancy business and could keep an interesting conversation about it going in the pub for all of, say 10 seconds. I could certainly talk for longer but unfortunately the 'interesting' aspect had a very short lifespan. Fortunately, I was aware of this so usually kept it short(ish)! The business is part of a national franchise, which is an approach I do recommend for those starting up a business…oh, my 10 seconds are now up.

I worked far more hours than was healthy. My food 'discipline' was at best patchy and, unsurprisingly, I was significantly overweight and very unfit. Seventeen-and-a-half stone was not good, especially for someone who needed to stretch to reach 5'11" on the height chart. I have always had a large frame, but not enough of one to justify that particular reading on the scales. Exercise had become a very distant memory, aside from the periodic scaling of the south face of the staircase, which seemed to be getting steeper as I got older. Personally, I put it down to global warming.

In short, I was the perfect fit for the middle-aged male stereotype, apart from the mid-life crisis, which, of course, didn't apply to me. Having said that, I had recently acquired a new car – a shiny Saab 9-3 Convertible, but this was purely a coincidence, of course!

It was a beautiful metallic electric blue, which I admit isn't the most masculine of colours, but I didn't care, although it soon became clear that others may have felt otherwise.

Just after it was delivered, I attended a family event and, as I pulled up outside, my brother Russell arrived just behind me. I stood next to my new pride and joy, waiting for the sibling admiration and to finally get the acknowledgement that I was now actually 'cool'.

He took one look at my car and, following a brief pause, said with his usual acerbic wit, "So, how long have you been a hairdresser then?" And so I spent the next four years with my car being referred to as 'Vidal Sassoon, the Hairdresser's Saab'. Thanks very much, brother.

Despite this, I was very happy with the car. As I was single, the first question my friends would always ask was whether it was a 'pussy magnet', to which my reply was, "It is until I get in it!" Unfortunately, all it took was a look in the mirror to realise there was way too much truth in this. My days of feline magnetism were clearly behind me and I just got on with life.

What's Up, Doc?

As they say, all long journeys start with the first step. And in this case the first step involved a trip in 'Vidal Sassoon' to the doctor's. If you have a delicate disposition, or are about to have your dinner, then you might want to come back to this chapter a bit later.

I had developed a condition, an extremely awkward condition. Let's just say that I had extreme soreness in the... let's call it the gentleman's area.

How sore? Well, enough that it glowed red like the rear brake lights of a Ford Focus and I was convinced I was passing sulphuric acid instead of urine. My friends thought that I was becoming emotionally sensitive, as they frequently caught me with a tear in the corner of my eye. Little did they know that I had just been to the gents to have my regular blowtorching of the todger, or at least that's how it felt. I liked referring to my little friend as "the dragon", but that was only because it really did breathe fire.

So I resorted to my preferred method of dealing with medical issues. This was to wait until the condition had cleared up on its own. However, after several months with no improvement, I was beginning to wear out my tear ducts and resigned myself to the dreaded trip to my GP's surgery.

As you can probably tell, this is not something I would do unless it was absolutely necessary. Sitting for hours in a doctor's waiting room full of people carrying every germ known to mankind had very little appeal. It's pretty high up on my list of things that are only marginally more enjoyable than receiving a knitting needle in the eye.

Just to make this extremely awkward situation even more embarrassing, the three doctors at my surgery were all women. I do confess that this had caused me to prolong the 'let it get better on its own' approach, as I wasn't relishing the prospect of presenting my embarrassing appendage to anyone, let alone a member of the opposite sex. I knew they were professionals, but they were also still women.

However, the glow had got brighter and the 'acid' passing stronger. I simply couldn't put it off any longer, so I threw in the towel and made the dreaded booking.

I arrived five minutes before the appointment, waited the prerequisite 90-minutes 'late' time and tried really hard not to reveal to the other patients how much discomfort I was in. Eventually my name was called. I entered the examination room and stood in front of the lady doctor with my head pointing downwards like a naughty six year old after being called to the headmaster for fighting in the playground. My bottom lip quivered and I completely avoided eye contact. I can only begin to imagine just how ridiculous this must have looked.

I finally summoned up the courage to state that I had a problem "in the lower regions".

Once we established that I wasn't talking about my ankles, or the Scottish Lowlands, the GP asked me to show her the problem. A voice in my head screamed, "What, you want to see it?" Whilst having a female show any interest in my private parts was usually very welcome (if not frequent), on this occasion that was definitely not the case and I really wanted my privates to stay just that! But this wasn't going to be possible, and things soon went from bad to worse.

I am sure that just as there have been for me, there have been occasions when you have meant to say one thing but proceeded to come out with words that although were similar sounding, meant something completely different. As the offending item was now VERY sore, I felt it necessary to warn the doctor of the unpleasant sight she was about to witness. But instead of saying the intended, "I am afraid it's not very pleasant," what I actually came out with was, "I am afraid it's not very impressive!" I knew what I meant.

There was a moment's silence. The GP stared right at me and with a straight face responded, "I am here to examine it, not to admire it." In that moment my embarrassment was complete. I had no choice but to drop my trousers and face the humiliation.

During the examination, I waited for the ground to open up and swallow me, but unfortunately this didn't happen. During the diagnosis, I definitely heard something about having an infection, but the subsequent questions that followed were all a bit of a blur, despite the fact that I seemed to provide adequate answers to them all. However, what I certainly did hear the doctor say was, "I am fairly certain that you have type 2 diabetes." Of all the things I thought could be responsible for a very sore member, diabetes was certainly not on that list. Apparently though, I ticked all of the high-risk categories, such as being over 40 (true), overweight (guilty m'lord) and having other family members with diabetes (my mum). On top of this, I apparently had all the typical symptoms of type 2 diabetes, such as tiredness, excessive thirst, drinking excessive amounts of water and the consequential increase in visits to the toilet. I had put all of this down to getting older.

To say that I was shocked at this diagnosis is an understatement. I had heard of diabetes, but this was an old person's illness and in my head I certainly wasn't old. I had lived by the mantra that growing old is mandatory but growing up is optional, and mentally I was still in my 20s. Unfortunately, though, my body was now in its late 40s and it was time to (reluctantly) face that fact. The bottom had just fallen out of my world, so I headed for home for a full-on dose of feeling sorry for myself.

Back to Earth

Back in the safe confines of my house, I headed up to my office (bedroom three) to sit and wallow in copious amounts of self-pity. I also logged on to the internet to find out as much as I could about this dreaded, life-limiting disease called diabetes.

Finding out that there were potential complications, such as heart disease, impotence, kidney failure, impotence, blindness, impotence, amputations, impotence and even death did not exactly reassure me. You might have realised by now that being a typical bloke, I was actually more alarmed by the possibility of impotence than the prospect of death. At least with death I wouldn't have to worry about a lack of stiffness!

The key word in all of this was 'potential', but of course that didn't fit with my mental state of impending doom and so that minor point was completely filtered out by my brain. I sat and thought, "This is awful, how could it be any worse?" Well, it didn't take long for me to get an answer to that question.

Fighting to convince myself there was a point to doing any work, I reluctantly opened up my email account. As I did so, I silently asked, "Why me? Why do I always have the bad luck? What have I done to deserve this?" I wanted to scream out loud, "It is not fair!"

Of course, I was being a complete and total pillock and was about to discover this in a very big way.

The very first email I opened was from the franchise's head office. The subject of the email was simply, "Tim". The only Tim I knew was a colleague and good friend who I knew had been battling cancer. I thought it was a battle that he had been winning, but unfortunately the email was to inform me that Tim had passed away the night before. I was devastated.

As part of the same national franchise, Tim and I had worked together training new recruits, which is how we got to know each other. Every couple of months we ran courses together at head office and had become good pals.

It was an incident during a meeting back in 2004 that gives me the warmest memory of Tim. All four trainers had a meeting with head office staff to review the training plans for the following year. Before proceedings began, we politely switched off our mobile phones and put them away in our pockets. Only William, one of our fellow trainers, left his on the table.

At the end of the meeting, we stayed put to have our lunch and catch up. As we chatted, William picked up his phone and switched it on. He punched in his four-digit security code and when this was rejected he tried again, with the same result. For those of you who don't remember, in the days before smartphones you had three attempts to enter your code before it was locked on the mobile network. The only way you could unlock it was to obtain a new code from the network provider, which usually involved a quest that Bilbo Baggins would have thought hard about before accepting. It was an extremely frustrating experience and one to be avoided at all costs. I liken it to Oliver with his begging bowl asking for more…at least that's what it felt like!

William, therefore, entered the code again extremely carefully, only for it to be rejected for a third time. The phone's chastity belt was now well and truly locked. William was clearly not happy, but of course we all found it absolutely hilarious, especially Tim who had been sitting next to him. He guffawed loudly in a most uncharitable way. We weren't revelling in William's misfortune, just the funny way he reacted to his apparent 'error'.

We only stopped laughing when we heard a phone ringing, though it wasn't clear where it was coming from. Just then, William pulled out a ringing mobile from his inside jacket pocket, which was identical to the locked one on the table. It was then we realised that the locked phone wasn't William's.

William then slid the frustration-inducing phone across the desk to Tim and said, "I think this is yours."

I have never seen someone's expression go from hilarity to total disbelief so quickly, as Tim realised that this was actually his phone. This gave the rest of us another reason to fall about laughing.

I was contemplating the fact that the news of Tim's passing meant things HAD actually got worse, when a completely unexpected thought occurred to me.

"I bet Tim's wife wished he only had diabetes."

In that moment, I realised that I wasn't unlucky to have diabetes; I was lucky to *only* have diabetes. It was a condition that I could choose to manage, and unfortunately Tim never had the chance to manage his illness. This revelation changed my whole outlook on my condition and how I went on to deal with it. I realised that my life wasn't over just yet and I spent the next couple of years managing my diabetes, not perfectly, but enough to keep the medical professionals involved in treating me reasonably happy.

I was prescribed medication in tablet form, which meant I didn't have to have the dreaded insulin injections I'd heard about. I also made dietary changes, which weren't as much of a hardship as they can be for others, as I have never really had a sweet tooth so giving up sugar was not a problem. Carbohydrates, however, were another matter entirely and moderation became the key word and my biggest challenge.

I made regular visits to my designated diabetes nurses to check all was in order and these were quite pleasant and completely stress-free. I took heed of the three key points – "diet, medication and regular exercise" – but only in the context of two out of three ain't bad. I kept meaning to start the exercise bit, but always seemed too busy.

There were changes in my life, but they were nowhere near as catastrophic as I'd feared. Most importantly, the nuclear todger was no more!

The Gang

In the first quarter of 2009, things in my life took an unexpected turn. I was in the very early stages of a new relationship with a lady called Susan. Since my divorce, I hadn't been particularly successful with the romantic side of my life, but I was quite optimistic this time.

I met Susan on an internet dating site and following a prolonged period of email correspondence, we finally met up. We got on really well, with the only downside being the distance between us. I lived on the Suffolk/Norfolk border and she resided in the south of Essex. Consequently, as it was a two-hour journey to see each other, we usually reserved weekends for spending time together.

I was pleasantly surprised when Susan asked me if I fancied joining her and a few others for a weekend in Newcastle in the coming September. Not being one to turn down a fun weekend, particularly with my new friend, I said yes straight away. It never occurred to me to ask what it was all in aid of. I wasn't exactly familiar with Newcastle, but I knew enough to know it wouldn't be hard to get a pint or find some evening entertainment.

A week or so later, I asked Susan whether the plan would be to take some booze with us or get it up there. I was astonished when her reply was, "Oh, they won't be drinking, at least not until Sunday evening." Fearing I was being subjected to a significant leg-pull, I enquired as to why. "They are doing the Great North Run," came the reply. I waited for the guilty grin to appear but unfortunately Susan's serious look remained. "You don't have to do it," she said. "I just thought you might like to come with me and cheer them on." I waited but there was no grin forthcoming and I realised my new girlfriend really was serious.

So, my involvement was to stand with Susan on the side of the road with a pint in my hand ready to cheer on her friends as they jogged by. I knew I could handle that, so the plan was good with me.

A few days later, I was introduced to the Newcastle party down the pub. I had mentally prepared myself for meeting a group of athletic types, but this wasn't the case at all – they were just ordinary people like me. The guys weren't far off my age, were carrying a little excess weight and didn't look as if exercise played a significant part in their daily life.

I know this sounds like the pot calling the kettle black, but I know I don't look like an athlete, so there's no surprise when I see myself in the mirror. But for some reason I thought that these guys would be super fit. Susan hadn't mentioned they were normal people.

Unfortunately, the conversation didn't quite go as I had expected.

"So, how many of you are actually doing the run?" I asked them.

"All of us," came the reply.

"Do any of you actually do any running?" I enquired, only to be astonished when I was told no, but they had just started training. I was trying to work out if drinking pints was part of the training schedule.

Out of the six unfit 40-something men around the table, I was the only one who wouldn't be taking part. My initial reaction was, "That's fine with me." But it didn't take long for it to dawn on me that on the big day I would be left to stand around like a total wet lemon while showing Susan's friends (and her) that I completely lacked the balls to do what they were doing. OK, so I was older than them, but that wasn't a plausible enough excuse. My Zimmer frame hadn't arrived just yet and this damn pride was now getting out of control.

I was managing it, just about, until I saw the look on Susan's face. As she listened to her friends explaining their plans, I could see the admiration she had for what they were doing. I know this is petty and extremely childish, but I just couldn't help thinking how much I really wanted her to feel that same kind of admiration for me.

I didn't want to go down in the estimation of my new girlfriend, which meant I now faced a serious dilemma. I desperately looked for a way out, but one that didn't involve the obvious option to join her friends on the run.

Stalling for time, I asked, "So, how do you go about entering the Great North Run?"

"You have to apply for a place in the ballot, but that closed a couple of months ago," one of them replied.

I spotted my opportunity. "So, is it too late to get a place in the ballot?"

"Yes," was the answer.

I managed to maintain an expression of disappointment whilst doing cartwheels inside. I had been handed an absolute gift that would allow me to save face, and I grasped it with both hands. I proudly stated, "Oh, that is a shame, I would have loved to have done the race with you guys." This of course was a total lie, but it allowed me to bathe in Susan's surprise and admiration.

It is actually very difficult to look disappointed when you are the smuggest person on the planet, but I actually pulled it off and got out of jail, or so I thought. After a brief pause, someone piped up, "You can get a charity place, as there will be plenty of those left."

I really hoped I had imagined this, but the expectant look on the faces of my new friends dispelled any chance of that. I tried to look happy whilst dwelling on the fact that people with good ideas are not always a good thing. I had backed myself into a corner and had no choice but to agree to take a charity place. I can't think of a time when I had so much trouble swallowing my beer. I had stated "That's great!" when

"Oh, bugger!" was the thought I couldn't get out of my head.

I was getting the look of admiration from Susan I'd so desired, and I was soon to discover the price I'd have to pay for it.

The Great North Run

And so I did the only thing that my out-of-control ego would let me do and signed up for a charity place. I chose to run for Diabetes UK, not just because I had the condition, but also for my late mum who had passed away the year before at the age of 80. As she also had diabetes, it was the obvious choice.

Once my entry was confirmed, it occurred to me that I ought to find out what this Great North Run thing was all about. I had seen it mentioned on the TV, but had never taken much notice. I guess in hindsight, doing some investigation before putting in my entry would have been sensible, but it was too late for that now.

My belated research revealed some interesting facts. The Great North Run is the largest half-marathon in the world. Approximately 50,000 people enter it every year, which sounded amazing.

I also discovered that it went from Newcastle to South Shields along the A194. Now, my knowledge of 'Northern' geography wasn't that good, but even I could work out that any run that went from one town to another was likely to be a long way, especially for me.

As it happens, it is 13.1 miles – to be precise. After an initial "HOW FAR???" followed by "YOU HAVE GOT TO

BE KIDDING!" it dawned on me this was half the distance of the London Marathon. Perhaps that is why they called it a half-marathon...doh! My feeling of total stupidity was increasing by the minute.

Now, I am sure there are many of you who think a half-marathon is not that bad. Well, that is probably because you bear a passing resemblance to an athlete and possess a degree of fitness.

Unfortunately, I was a UFO. No, I wasn't an extra-terrestrial being, although there are some people who are not totally convinced of this, but I was most definitely a UFO in the context that I was extremely **U**nfit, very **F**at and too **O**ld! The Great North Run was definitely not the place for a decrepit UFO to start his running career.

This view was confirmed when my research revealed that in almost 30 years of the Great North Run, 13 people had actually died taking part and four of them had lost their lives in the same race only four years earlier. There had to be easier ways to commit suicide!

"What the hell had I done?"

There have been many occasions in history when a man has laid down his life for a woman, and it looked like I could be the next.

I was a UFO with a mountain to climb.

Top Gear

I think it's fair to say that a number of factors had made me embark on this journey. Firstly, my desire not to look like a total pilchard in front of Susan had caused me to throw my hat into the ring…well, it was more of a straight, long dual carriageway than a ring. But in hindsight, I shouldn't have been anywhere near the ring, let alone close enough to throw anything into it.

What little face-saving relief I felt soon evaporated. It dawned on me that any personal credibility I'd saved by entering the race would be lost when on the day itself I'd show myself to be a complete UFO. This depressing thought was replaced by the desire just to survive and not become statistic number 14.

In order to get more than 100 yards from the start line before collapsing into the arms of the nearest St John Ambulance volunteer and their defibrillator, I clearly needed to train. I'd consider it a bonus if I was able to do anything more than this.

As for the training, I am not sure if I was more concerned by getting out and 'pounding the streets' or the looks and sniggers I would get as I did so. I lived in the small town of Brandon in Suffolk, which had lots of through traffic, so there would always be an unwelcome audience with nothing better to do than stare at passers-by while they waited in the lengthy queue at the traffic lights.

If I was going to be an athlete and command their respect, then I had to look the part. So, off I went to a running shop in Norwich to kit myself out with all the right gear.

I can remember the specific point when I realised this was a shop for serious runners. It was the moment shortly after I walked through the door, when the assistant raised his eyebrow as he gathered I was looking for something for me and not a present for someone else. He did well to maintain his warm, friendly smile, but I could tell it was becoming harder and harder to uphold. I wasn't sure if there was a contemptuous thought behind that grin, along the lines of, "Oh, God, not another one!" Looking back, I actually believe it was guilt, the sort that any decent person would feel as they helped an old man into the barrel just upstream from Niagara Falls. The sales assistant was now complicit in whatever self-inflicted harm I was about to carry out. Despite this, he tended to my needs as any professional would. He provided all of the required kit, and what was really amazing was that it did actually come in my size, even if it was kept on a separate rail right at the back of the store. I might have been shopping from the Fat Bastard Rail, but to me it looked as good as the smaller sizes. I was also measured up for some serious running shoes and even purchased a GPS running watch that measured distance, speed and lots of other apparently important stuff. The only thing it lacked was the obvious, "You gotta be kidding" indicator, although I suspect I was well up this scale already. However, I was now ready to become an athlete, and so I headed for home to prepare for my first training run.

It was with great pride that I donned my new uniform and prepared to face the world. I was no longer a fat old bloke – I was an athlete. After some warm-ups, I stepped out of the front door and strolled towards the end of my cul-de-sac. I eagerly anticipated the respectful looks as my new athletic-self showed how it should be done. I broke into a jog, puffed out my chest with pride and set off to accept the praise and respect I deserved.

Well, that was the plan, but the stares from the surrounding car occupants were accompanied either by open-mouthed disbelief or plain hilarity. My first thought was that there must be something really funny on the radio and what a coincidence it was that all the cars were tuned into the same station. Then it dawned on me how unlikely it was that everyone was listening to the same humorous broadcast. There must be some other reason for their smiles.

It wasn't so much the sound of a penny dropping, but the noise of a very large boulder hitting a concrete floor. Not surprisingly, it soon became clear that a fat old bloke in running gear looks like…a fat old bloke in running gear! I had created a serious contender for the 'What On Earth Was I Thinking?' award.

Training

I needed to get in some serious training if I was to avoid the embarrassment of letting Susan and her friends down, so I had no choice but to persevere through the inevitable humiliation. Or, more correctly, my ego didn't want to show what a lame, over-the-hill loser I was.

I would just have to give some careful consideration to where and when I did my training runs. I lived right on the edge of Thetford Forest, and so that seemed an ideal place to start some discreet jogging. However, there were a couple of issues with this.

Firstly, although there weren't many people in the forest, there was something far worse. I had not prepared myself for the rude, judgemental, sarcastic…deer.

I know what you are thinking; that the painful experience with the car occupants had left me paranoid, but you didn't see the deer. As I passed by they gave me a look of total disbelief, their eyes and even their antlers seemed disapproving. I could almost hear one say, "Hey, Bert, look at the pillock heading this way!"

In addition, the early sunset made an after-work run totally impossible, as running in a forest in the dark is a definite health hazard. If you could manage to avoid running straight into one of the many trees, you would almost certainly end up face down in the dirt after tripping over the difficult-to-see tree roots that criss-crossed the path. And yes, I know because this is exactly what happened to me as dusk approached. And so the fat old bloke in running gear managed to make himself even more of a source of amusement when, just as a group of teenagers came flying around the corner, he became a fat old bloke in running gear lying face down in the dirt. Need I say more? I don't think so, as we all know how sensitive teenagers are to avoiding other people's embarrassment (or not)!

So I decided that for the time being I needed to stick to the roads. I managed to find a route that mostly involved backstreets that were lit so that I could run later in the day while avoiding the busy periods. With my new strategy decided upon, it was time to make a proper start to my training regime.

Unfortunately, there are many things in life that allow you to become delusional about your abilities and prevent you from realising just how far you are from where you really need to be. This does not go on for very long when you are a UFO who has just taken up running. In fact, you very quickly become aware of your limitations.

I should have started to realise this when prior to my first run, the simple task of stretching muscles caused a significant increase in my breathing and heart rate. Initially, I put this down to excitement and anticipation, but I soon realised that it was solely because of how ridiculously unfit I was. Not only was I scraping the bottom of my barrel of capability, the barrel had a serious hole in the bottom of it.

On my first proper 'run', I thought of the advice the assistant in the running shop had given me. "At the beginning, run a short distance and then walk a similar distance, and so on," he'd said. I completed the first 'run' with the emphasis on short. I wasn't able to complete the walking part as I was doubled over, gasping for breath and listening to my heart pounding like the cannons from the finale of the 1812 overture. I was in a bad way. It seemed I hadn't gone more than a few hundred yards before making myself a candidate for the Cardiac Department of West Suffolk Hospital.

This was going to be harder than I thought, but my initial desire to come to my senses, accept my limitations and throw in the towel was soon replaced by the egotistic fear of losing face in front of Susan. If there was one thing I had learnt from all of this, it was that dating in your 40s is really hard work!

So I had no choice but to persevere and repeat the whole training exercise four times a week. After a fortnight of my main objective being to make sure I stopped before the heart attack started, I began to notice a small change. Slowly and gradually I was able to increase my distance and reduce the walking element. Of course, I was able to measure all of this on my fancy watch, but up to this point I could have used the calendar hanging on my kitchen wall.

Soon I was able to jog for a whole mile without any walking. The fear of a coronary was subsiding and despite breathing difficulties and muscle aches, I was noticing an improvement, which spurred me on.

However, any possibility of my self-belief getting out of control was soon to be curbed. One evening, on one of my one-mile training 'runs' on a long backstreet well away from public attention, I saw a lady emerge from a garden gate with a pushchair and proceed in the same direction as me. Now, this would be a first, as although I had passed pedestrians going in the other direction from me (usually with a pained expression as they tried to suppress their mirth), this was to be the first time I would pass someone heading in the same direction. Under the circumstances, it was important to retain as much self-respect as possible and minimise any sniggering. I concentrated hard on my running technique and, more importantly, tried to regulate my breathing so that it sounded more like controlled inhalations rather than the gasping of a man taking his last breaths on this earth, which was more usual.

It wasn't easy to achieve both, but I concentrated harder than ever before and eventually felt I had both my technique and breathing relatively under control. It was now time for an accomplished and stylish overtake.

Unfortunately, it was at this point I noticed the woman and pushchair were actually further away from me than before. I was hit by the realisation that she was actually walking faster than I was running – I couldn't even keep up with a woman with a pushchair.

In this moment I realised the term 'jogging' was far more appropriate when applied to me than 'running'. The size of the challenge I'd signed up to seemed even bigger.

I decided I needed to be motivated by distance targets rather than time-based ones. Looking back, this was actually a wise thing to do and something that would prove beneficial later on.

Meet the Parents

Despite the disappointment of discovering that I had all the speed of a paraplegic snail, my new-found strategy of concentrating solely on distance rather than pace was actually paying off and it wasn't that long before I found myself regularly completing three to four-mile distances.

It was around this time that my relationship with Susan went to the next level. We had been seeing each other for about six months and she felt it was time for me to meet the parents, a prospect that I found intimidating, even in my late 40s. In fact, it was probably even worse, as I understood the importance of making a good first impression far more than I did when I was a teenager meeting my ex-wife's family for the first time. Looking back to my time as a spotty apprentice, complete with motorcycle, I had all the social awareness of a vendor selling bacon sandwiches outside a mosque in Riyadh. I guess the fact I was so ignorant at the time made me oblivious to what sort of impression I was making.

But that was then, and now I had accumulated enough awareness of social etiquette not to make those mistakes again. However, this awareness did bring a degree of nervousness that would have been far more appropriate in a teenager. I really did have a significant degree of trepidation about this meeting. Susan had arranged for a nice Sunday lunch at her Billericay home, where I would meet her parents and grown-up children, Aimee and Sam.

In the morning, it became obvious that my nervous state was rubbing off on Susan and affecting her cooking concentration. She is a wonderful cook and her desire to dish up a superb spread for her guests was as important to her as making a good first impression was to me.

She was clearly finding the prospect of me hanging around being a nuisance something she needed to curtail. It got to the point where she was rambling on about something in a manner I just didn't understand. She seemed to be talking about respiratory problems being caused by animal skin. Her exact words were, "Why don't you just **fur cough** and go for a run?"

This was lost on me, as my throat was absolutely fine, but I did get the bit about going for a run. That seemed the perfect way to get rid of all the pent-up energy that was making me so irritable. I had enough time to train for a while then shower and change before the guests arrived.

I put on my running gear, completed my warm-ups and headed off to tackle the streets of Billericay. It turned out to be a good run, as I completed a personal best of five miles, which I can only put down to the extra adrenalin pumping around my body. As I finished I felt good, if a bit tired and extremely red in the face. I was a vision to behold, not only because of my colour but also due to the fact that the extremely cold snap we were having meant I was wearing running tights under my shorts. However, this wasn't going to be a problem as I had time to shower and change before I had my parental audience.

Imagine then my reaction as I came around the final corner to Susan's house to see a Toyota Corolla on her driveway with her father opening the driver's door. They weren't supposed to be here yet! I was going to have to meet them looking like a knackered Superman with sunburn. This was not the first impression I was looking to make.

I thought about turning around and finding another way into the house, but soon realised this just wasn't possible. I had no choice but to face them as I was. I told myself to try and appear confident and charming, although I knew this was going to require a performance worthy of an Oscar nomination. As Susan's father exited the car, I strode up to him and introduced myself. He looked me up and down, surprised at the vision before him. When his eyebrows had finally come down from the significant altitude they had risen to, he said, "Ello, son" in his really strong Essex accent. At least it was polite and not the "F*** me" I was expecting, and he was no doubt thinking. After shaking hands, I turned to address Susan's mother Jean and saw that she was still sitting in the car.

I realised Jean had refrained from exiting the vehicle because she had a baking dish on her lap, which had a lid on the top and a tea towel underneath. In the dish was an apple crumble that she had baked for the lunch. What I failed to realise at the time (but have been reminded about by Susan many times since) is that the production of the crumble involved her mother dragging her father away from the cricket to go and buy the apples, which resulted in him missing the conclusion of the England Ashes victory over Australia. I believe at some time during the shopping he may have uttered the phrase, "This bloke had better be worth it," although the number of times he did so is still not clear. No pressure then.

But this was my opportunity to apply the charm. I gallantly opened the car door and introduced myself. All I needed was a puddle and a cloak and my Sir Walter Raleigh impression would have been complete. But all I had was a baking dish and a tea towel. So I offered to take it from Jean so that she could get out of the car. She handed it over with a very clear "Be careful with it" instruction.

I took it from her and, as the dish was still hot, carefully held it on the tea towel to avoid burning my hands, as I definitely wouldn't want to drop it. I walked to the front door and stared up at the doorbell, which some idiot had fitted above eye level. I looked back to see Terry doing something with the contents of his car boot while Jean was still getting out of the car.

I could either stand there looking even more like a lemon, shout like an old washerwoman to get Susan's attention or find a way to ring that bell.

It was then that I made a very, very, very bad decision. I decided to reach up with the baking dish and press the bell with the back of my hand. This shouldn't have been a problem, as I was holding on very tightly, but what I hadn't considered was that I was actually holding onto the tea towel, not the dish. As I reached the summit of my stretching, the baking dish slowly slid off the towel like an ocean liner being launched into the sea. I can still recall the slow-motion sequence of the dish heading towards the floor. In that brief moment, I prayed for an outcome that involved the dish bouncing and landing upright with the crumble intact. But, of course, that didn't happen, and it didn't matter which way it landed, as it smashed onto the doorstep, spreading apple crumble and pieces of bakeware up the wall, across the driveway and up the front of the Toyota Corolla. I looked down in horror at the carnage around me.

I forced myself to look up and saw Jean standing at the end of the driveway. She was completely motionless with her mouth wide open. She stood like this, not uttering a word, for what seemed an eternity. I was in a state of complete distress, as my gaze went back and forth between Jean and the floor. Each time I looked up she had not moved at all. Had it not been for the fact she was standing up, you might have thought that the shock had killed her.

As I bent down and frantically tried to salvage something of the mess on the floor (a ridiculous gesture I now appreciate), Terry strode up the driveway. As he reached me, I tried to say I was sorry, but the trauma wouldn't let any words come out. Terry put his hand on my shoulder and in his deep Essex accent uttered a phrase that I will never forget. In a reassuring manner he stated, "Don't worry about it, son, I f***ing hate crumble."

This is a line I have laughed at many times since, but I didn't at the time as the humour of the moment was lost on me, especially as Jean was still standing next to the car doing her waiting-for-the-dentist statue impression. Feeling this moment couldn't get any worse, Terry proved me wrong when he told me that the dish belonged to Jean's grandmother and was very precious to her. I was devastated, felt awful and went off to change. If the toilet bowl had been any bigger, I would definitely have flushed myself down it.

Despite the catastrophic start, we did enjoy a very nice lunch, although everyone insisted on stating how much they had been looking forward to Jean's crumble. "Crumble's Off" became the catchphrase of the day. I found the mirth a little difficult, as I was still feeling bad about having smashed the family heirloom. However, it became clear to me just how much they were yanking my chain when Aimee's boyfriend Steve whispered to me, "Do you really think they had Pyrex in the 19th century?"

This was the first of the many times I would encounter Terry's wonderful dry wit. Fortunately, the only damage done was to the Pyrex dish, which, of course, I would later replace.

Tearing It Up

Having survived my ordeal, I managed to continue with my training schedule, which wasn't going too badly until a couple of days off changed all that.

Susan and I spent a weekend in the New Forest attending the wedding of my nephew, David, and his other half, Michelle. What was so good about this was that my new-found fitness and stamina meant that at the reception I could let the other attendees enjoy my well-honed 'Dad Dancing' for a far longer period than usual, and with so much more vigour. Oh, lucky them. It was a really good night and we stayed over in a local hotel with other family members.

On the Sunday we decided to spend some time in the pretty town of Lyndhurst and have some lunch before heading home. On this sunny and pleasant summer's day, we sat at a table outside the Mailman's Arms, where we enjoyed a bite to eat, a little liquid refreshment and indulged in plenty of people watching. It wasn't quite the Champs Elysees, but in some ways it was even more entertaining, as the combination of Brits and summer wear often provides a good opportunity to raise a smile.

After this we decided to join those we had been gawping at and have a walk up the high street to have a browse. At the far end of the street we entered a shop and marvelled at the dazzling array of crap that tourists lap up. The thought, "Do people really buy this stuff?" definitely occurred to me more than once. And the answer was "Yes, they do", as an American tourist got very excited at finding a model of the Eiffel Tower adorned with our Union Jack. I just didn't have the heart to tell him the geographical error, as he seemed so pleased with his find.

Whilst I stood in awe admiring the 'tat-selling' that would have had Alan Sugar positively aroused, I put my hand in my pocket. This had nothing to do with feeling like Alan Sugar, it was just to get my mobile phone, which I discovered wasn't there. My Blackberry was missing too.

I panicked and first decided I had been the victim of some techno-freak pickpocket that had no interest in silly stuff like wallets, money or credit cards. Once I had dismissed this ridiculous idea, I then realised that I had left them at the pub…on the table outside…near the high street pavement… where everyone was passing. They had both probably gone by now.

I ran out of the shop and legged it as fast as I could down the high street. And this time I was not jogging, I was sprinting, and the looks I was attracting were more in admiration than the ridicule I had become accustomed to. As I reached a running speed that I had not been capable of for at least the previous 25 years, a bizarre thought entered my head. My initial panic was now replaced by a warm glow of self-confidence. I really was running, and I was running very fast. I was fit, confident and impressive. I do have to confess that I had an image in my head of the beach scene from '*Chariots of Fire*'. The Vangelis theme played loudly in my head until it was halted by a sensation that I can only liken to someone using a heavy-duty chainsaw on the back of my calf muscle.

The pain was off the scale, as I had managed to tear the muscle; quite badly, I was later to find out. There now followed a battle in my brain, as one side of it insisted that I fall on the floor and whimper like a child whilst the other side kept reminding me of the mobile phone and Blackberry. And so I managed the most ungracious of compromise solutions, which was to hop on the good leg whilst whimpering like a child. The looks I received as I completed the journey to the pub were now not quite so full of admiration, and the general consensus seemed to be a toss up between laughing and feeling pity. I do believe that some people even managed both.

The only good thing to come out of it was that surprisingly I did get my devices back, as some kind soul had handed them over to the landlord. Susan helped me to hop back to the car, as I couldn't even walk. I knew that this was something far more serious than a pulled muscle. As Susan drove us home, I reflected on the fact that my preparations for the Great North Run were now in tatters. I was a UFO with a serious injury.

Now, the astute amongst you will no doubt have already realised that I had actually been handed a real opportunity. I now had the perfect excuse to withdraw from the race without any loss of pride whatsoever. I no longer had to risk the pain, torture and humiliation that fun runners subject themselves to. I no longer had to put myself through the training regime and, more importantly, I no longer had to face the risk of becoming fatality number 14! I could quit with my head held high and Susan wouldn't think any less of me.

There was only one problem – I didn't want to.

As unlikely as it sounds, until that moment I hadn't realised I had actually got the bug, and not the flu type. I never thought I would feel so disappointed at the prospect of giving up running. So many times I had wanted it to end and then, when I had the chance to pack it in, I realised I actually needed it. I can only liken it to someone missing their sexually transmitted disease after the penicillin has kicked in – I definitely didn't see that one coming.

I guess I had focused so much on the end goal that I couldn't just let go of it. I had come so far and was now desperate to see it through, even though time was running out – the day of the race was only a few weeks away.

Patching it Up

I remembered how the running shop in Norwich, where I had bought my kit, had a treatment room and a dedicated Sports Injury Therapist. Earlier in his career, he had been involved with the England athletics team. I went to see him, as my insistence on being determined/pig-headed/plain stupid (delete as appropriate) meant that the sensible option of resting the injury for a few months was no longer a solution.

The therapist was a nice guy and had all of the skills and qualities required to help me...apart from one. An injury of this nature was not only sore when walking but was also extremely painful to the touch. Even putting on socks and trousers was a serious challenge, as any contact resulted in a scream. Not very manly I admit, but the agony was intense. Consequently, what was needed was an empathetic and gentle technique from someone that was sensitive to the pain being caused. Not a chance! This was brutal stuff and I had not suffered that much pain since my divorce. I am confident that if you go back now and check the treatment table, you will still find my teeth marks in it. If there is ever a need to check my dental records, then this is the place to go. Despite this, I have to say that he worked wonders and whilst an overnight cure was totally unrealistic, he certainly speeded up the recovery process.

After several treatments, I was told I had to rest it for 10 days before resuming very gentle training. This was too long as far as I was concerned and so we settled on seven days and then some not-so-gentle training. Well, when I say "settled", I should point out that this conversation was just with me after I had left the sports shop. He would only have shouted at me, and no doubt for good reason. But not for the first time in my life, I was sure that I knew best. And, like so many other times, this was not the case.

Cyprus Break

As my training schedule was on hold, I decided to take advantage of the situation and have a short break and get away for a few days. This is one of the advantages of working for yourself, and my boss tends to be quite accommodating.

I decided that I would get some short notice flights and take Susan to see my friend Dianne (better known as Di), who lived and worked in Nicosia in Cyprus. Di and I had been good friends for some time before she buggered off abroad, but we had kept in touch.

It was on this short visit that an incident happened which had nothing to do with running, but it always makes me smile just thinking about it, as this is exactly how it happened.

We landed at Larnaca Airport in the early evening and I picked up a hire car; a fairly ordinary, run-of-the-mill, medium-sized black hatchback that was just like any other medium-sized hatchback.

We arrived at Di's flat at about 9pm. As we hadn't eaten I suggested we go get a take-out. Not far from Di's was my favourite ever delicatessen. They did a fantastic range of both hot and cold food at all hours of the day and night. I enjoyed eating from there just as much as going out for a meal. Plan agreed, the three of us jumped in the hire car and headed off to get some grub. I was in food heaven as our basket was filled.

We emerged after about 20 minutes with far more food than we could sensibly eat, which was quite traditional for me and part of the reason why I had become a UFO. Well, at least the Fat aspect of it. However, what was good was that I had moved on from the phase of "being a pig" to the phase of "taking on Carbs!" This had now become "It is to help my muscle recover." But everyone knew that I was still just being a pig.

As we left the store, the three of us turned the corner and walked past a number of parked cars before climbing into ours. I jumped in the driver's seat and Susan got in the front passenger seat. We then waited in vain for the rear door to open. After about 30 seconds, I began to wonder where Di was, as she had been walking with us just before we reached the car. As I turned to see if she was near the car door, I noticed a woman sitting in the back seat of the car next to us. What attracted my initial gaze was just how much she looked like Di. Then I realised – it was Di.

My initial curiosity of wondering why Di had got into that car instead of ours was soon forgotten when the lady in the driving seat started screaming hysterically as she realised a crazy woman had got into the back of her car. At the same time Di also started screaming hysterically due to her belief that some crazy woman had got into the front of our car. This went on for what seemed an eternity, although I suspect it was only seconds, as due to the shock both women seemed incapable of either moving or halting the screaming. It was then that Di spotted Susan and me laughing hysterically in the car next to her.

What was even funnier was how the look on Di's face changed from terror to confusion without any abatement of the screaming. She was obviously wondering why we had got into the wrong car AND why the crazy woman was in ours. Then the penny dropped, she stopped screaming, leapt out of the car and jumped into the back of ours. "DRIVE, DRIVE, DRIVE!" she barked in a way that would have made a bank robber proud. As I reversed out of the space, I just had time to see the other lady, who was still screaming, not quite so loudly, but now with the same confused expression that Di had demonstrated moments before.

We were still laughing as we finished our food. I have never seen Di that embarrassed before, or since. We often recall that day. Well, usually it's me who recalls it and laughs extensively while Di just glares. She has a great sense of humour and so I know she secretly chuckles about it. Well, I hope she does or she will kill me when she reads this chapter.

It was a great break, as any time spent with Di always is, and it really helped lift my spirits. As always, time went far too quickly and after a few days we had to head back to the UK.

Back to Training

Back home, I resumed training and went through several frustrating weeks as I pushed the muscle before it had sufficiently recovered. This, of course, resulted in a relapse, as the muscle objected to the abuse and delivered a sharp pain, which brought proceedings to a halt. After a few days' rest, my impatience invariably got the better of me and I repeated this uncomfortable cycle several times over.

When the last breakdown happened just three weeks before the day of the Great North Run, it was effectively all over. Well, it should have been, but I just wasn't prepared to give in. This was the moment that resulted in one of the most stupid decisions I have ever made, but one that I have no regrets over. I decided that I wasn't going to give up, and when the muscle gave in I'd just run through the pain. I knew my chances of finishing the race were zero, but I now had a new objective of just making the start line. Anything after that would be a bonus. Common sense was now a very rare commodity.

I went back to the shop and bought compression socks that came up to my knees and some neoprene calf muscle supports. Instead of making me look more professional, this new bit of kit just made me look like even more of a tit, but I didn't care. The days were getting longer so I could go back to training in Thetford Forest. The ground was softer than the concrete roads, which made things slightly easier on the painful muscle, and there were fewer people to laugh at the UFO with the contorted face. Just think of Quasimodo in running gear and you'll get the picture. At this point, there was no doubt that I was being 100% pig-headed. There wasn't a single person who agreed with what I was doing, but when you live on your own and your partner is almost 100 miles away, there isn't anyone to stop you. Even I knew it was wrong, but that wasn't going to stop me. I became even more focused on reaching my goal of taking part in the race.

For the next three weeks, I ran every other day. The pain would usually kick in just half a mile into the run, but despite this I managed to slightly extend my distance each time. The literature in my GNR starting pack was very clear and stated you should not do the race unless you had comfortably completed an eight-mile run during training. Well, the best I had managed so far was five miles, and this was anything but comfortable.

One part of me felt a sense of achievement that I had actually managed to run five whole miles, but I clearly wasn't in a good state for the race. I was now a UFO with a serious injury who had not completed enough training. It couldn't get any worse, could it?

Time had run out, but if little else I still intended to make the start line.

Getting Ready

On the weekend of the race, we all set off for the North East. The plan was to travel up on the Friday, relax on the Saturday, run on the Sunday and then travel back again on the Monday.

After an uneventful journey, we arrived at our accommodation – two adjacent cottages in a village just outside Durham.

Friday evening was a social affair, with the seven of us enjoying pleasant conversation, lots of humour and a very good Chinese takeaway. This was perfect for the job of stocking up on carbohydrates, a key point in preparing for the race. I have to confess, it was at this point I realised the very best thing about the Great North Run weekend was that it mainly consisted of guilt-free eating. Is there any better type of indulgence? I don't think so. It was all for a good cause and I was very happy to give that cause my full attention. Susan was an admirable supporter and she was even willing to help us with the Chinese – what a hero.

Saturday was an interesting day. After a full plate of carbs for breakfast we headed into Durham for the day, taking in the castle and the beautiful cathedral. It was a nice distraction from what was about to take place.

Between sightseeing, I did have to spend some time tracking down a pharmacy. The reason for this was something that I haven't mentioned so far. On this particular day, the day before the Great North Run, I developed my first case of – and not repeated since – haemorrhoids! Those of you unfortunate enough to have had this condition will understand how uncomfortable it can be, especially if you are planning to run a half-marathon the next day. I kid you not, of the 17,882 days I had spent on this planet, why did this one have to be the day I developed an uncomfortable and embarrassing condition?

I had definitely answered the previous question of: "It couldn't get any worse, could it?" I was now a UFO with a serious injury who had not completed enough training and had a dose of piles! From this point, the phrase "It can't get any worse" was banned from my vocabulary, as I seemed to keep finding ways to prove it to be untrue.

I remember reading that the most important thing in taking on the Great North Run is to ensure that you do the right preparation. And thanks to the chemist, I knew I did, as it was written in large letters on the tube…PREPARATION H!

My feelings of trepidation were now at maximum, and my sense of optimism couldn't have sunk any lower. I chose not to mention my condition to my fellow runners, as I am sure they were getting fed up of the endless list of excuses I'd already come out with.

I should also mention that up until this point, I had been very concerned about the dreaded nipple chafing I had heard so much about. Apparently, this can be really bad for men, with vest rubbing causing severe bleeding and pain. I'd heard that the way to avoid this is to apply Vaseline to your nipples before you start the race, reapplying it during the run by taking a dollop from one of the stewards, who I'd been told would be holding out jars of it at several key points along the route. I wasn't too keen on this, as I felt that rubbing your nipples as you run past a large crowd of spectators was way too perverted.

However, this thought was now replaced by the prospect of passing these same spectators as I applied a dose of cream up my arse. I can only imagine what they would make of that, especially if the other hand was rubbing a nipple at the same time. God help us all!

I managed to keep this thought to myself that evening, as we all enjoyed dining on my homemade Spaghetti Bolognese (lots of carbs!) before chilling out before the big event. It wasn't going to be a late night, as we had to be up very early the next day.

The Day

And so it was that at some unearthly hour on a Sunday morning in September, an alarm brought us back into the real world and the realisation of what was ahead of us.

A relatively light breakfast was the order of the day, as the thought of keeping it down overtook the need to store carbs. Avoiding throwing up on the side of a Tyne and Wear street in front of crowds of onlookers seemed a far more important prospect than filling up the energy tank. Besides, I was expecting the calf muscle to give out long before the energy levels did. After all, there isn't much point in ensuring the car fuel tank is full to the brim when the wheels are about to fall off. In this situation, running out of fuel is the least of your worries.

After a shower, it was time to start the proper preparation for the challenge ahead. I put on my running gear along with a sweatshirt over the top to cope with the early September morning chill, even though a pleasant day was forecast. I slapped on all the necessary creams and lotions, including a liberal application of Preparation H, which did make me wonder how many Olympic athletes have had to go through the same thing. To my calf muscles I applied an even more generous amount of Deep Heat, in an attempt to make them as supple as possible for the ordeal ahead. Fortunately, I didn't get the two creams mixed up, as that would have been really nasty. Mind you, putting Deep Heat up my arse would certainly have taken my mind off the calf muscle.

Now, those of you who are familiar with Deep Heat will know that its muscle-warming qualities are very good, unlike the smell which has to be one of the strongest and most unpleasant mankind has created. Let's just say that I put on enough to provoke cries and derogatory comments from those downstairs. And that was before I had even left the bedroom. I certainly couldn't be accused of not putting enough on, which was endorsed by the looks from the other runners at the start line several hours later. I can only liken it to the awkwardness that exists when you are responsible for an inadvertent fart in a crowded lift. Your companions may be pretty sure you're the one responsible for it, but they just can't prove it.

When everyone was ready, we jumped into our cars and headed for South Shields, which is where the finish line is located. It was a lovely sunny morning and despite the chill in the air it promised to be a nice day.

Having parked in one of the special car parks for the day, we all said farewell to Susan and I basked in the 'admiration kiss' she gave me. We then jumped onto one of the many special buses provided to take the runners to the start line. As we travelled towards Newcastle on a double decker, two thoughts occurred to me. The first was that I now had some sort of insight into how death row prisoners feel on their way to meet their fate. I kept expecting to hear a cry of "dead man walking," but it didn't happen. The second thought was that the bus would have been far more useful if it could have carried us from the start to the finish, and not the other way around. Apparently, that was not allowed – shame.

Once the bus reached its destination, we joined the masses pouring through the streets of Newcastle headed towards that single point. It was just like match day for a big football game. The only difference was that it was far less likely that a gang of rival supporters would be waiting around the corner to kick the crap out of us, which made me very happy indeed.

As we neared the start line, I experienced what an excess of 40,000 runners looks like. It was impossible not to be impressed. I was beginning to feel that I was part of something special, although my contribution was likely to be a very short one.

To give you an idea, the start line is on the A167, on the outskirts of Newcastle. It is a dual carriageway and all four lanes were in use. By the time the race was due to start, the volume of people stretched back over a kilometre. Now, to stop the obvious carnage that would inevitably ensue with a race involving runners with mixed abilities, all the runners were categorised. They were allocated a zone based on their expected finish time, with the fastest starting first and the slowest setting off last. I recall my entry form requiring an expected finish time. I only just resisted the temptation to put late September!

The folk in Zone A had yellow running numbers. These were the professional elite runners. A 'yellow' runner would almost certainly win the race. The runners in zones B, C and D sported orange numbers. These were the serious club runners who were used to competing at a high level. The people in zones E, F and G wore white numbers and were the less accomplished club runners or competent runners from the general public. Zones H and I were reserved for the green numbers – mainly fun runners. The people in zones J and K wore pink numbers and they could be categorised as "you're having a laugh". To be fair, most of them generally were.

Needless to say, when my entry pack arrived it included my number. Unsurprisingly, it was on a pink background. However, there was one item missing from my pack – the timing chip. This was a little electronic device – unique to each runner – that you strapped to your trainers. It would record the moment you crossed the start and finish lines, providing an exact personal time for the run.

I'd phoned the helpline to notify them of the missing chip, expecting them to send me another one. However, they said I would have to go to the information hut on the day, where they would swap my number for a new one, including a chip. So that is exactly what I did. Once I reached the front of the queue, I explained the situation, gave my details and handed over my number. In return they handed back a new number and an associated timing chip. I looked at the number and asked, "Are you sure about this?" to which they replied, "You just get whatever number comes next."

I sort of accepted this and pinned the number to my vest. The reason I had questioned it was the number was in fact an orange one. For those of you who have been paying attention, you will recall that the orange numbers were for the highly competitive, serious club runners.

If this wasn't enough of a surprise, you needed to actually witness the sight this number was now pinned to. I haven't yet mentioned the costume I had agreed to wear to promote Diabetes UK. It included, amongst other things, a pink wig.

To say that it was a little out of keeping with a typical 'orange' athlete is an understatement of major proportions, and it enabled a moment of mischief just too tempting to resist.

Virtually all of the runners were coming from the direction of the centre of Newcastle, which meant that everyone passed the actual start line as they travelled to their respective zones. For those of us at the back in the pink zone, that meant a one-kilometre walk. The runners began to congregate in the vicinity of their respective zones and commenced their warm-up rituals. As I passed the yellow zone, I tried and failed to spot famous runners, which I suspect was mostly to do with my complete ignorance of athletics over the previous few years.

It was when we got to the next zone that the devil in me broke free. I was officially an orange runner, so, much to the amusement of my compatriots, I marched right into the middle of these super-fit guys and began trying to replicate their warm-up routine. Initially, they seemed annoyed I had invaded their territory. One of them even began to move towards me. It was obvious he was about to bark an order in my direction, along the lines of, "What are you doing in here? Sod off to your own zone." However, just before he began to utter these words, his line of vision dropped, presumably so that he could tell me exactly which zone to sod off to. It was then he caught sight of my orange number, which resulted in his irritated expression being replaced by one that was a definite “does not compute”. This expression spread around the other serious runners in the zone. They obviously felt that I shouldn’t be there, but the orange number on my shirt prevented them from telling me so. For the next 10 minutes, I did my best to mimic their stretches and limbers, but I have to admit that even this proved quite a challenge for me. The strange looks I was getting from these guys was nothing compared to the smiles I was receiving from the less serious runners as they passed by.

When I got the call from my compatriots that we needed to go, I said loudly, “Have a good run, guys.” Bidding the orange boys and girls farewell, I headed off to my rightful position at the back.

The Start

I had to pinch myself to prove that I was finally here. I had made it to the start, which was the only realistic objective I had been able to set for myself under the circumstances, and I was happy. Well, I was now actually one-kilometre away from the start line, but I was quietly confident that I could make it that far. As we waited for the start time to arrive, there was a real party atmosphere. Music was playing through huge speakers and the 'pinkies' all laughed and joked with each other. I wasn't sure if they were all genuinely relaxed or if it was just nerves, but I suspect it was a bit of both.

I thought of everything I had gone through to get to this point, particularly what I had endured over the previous month. I was satisfied with what I had achieved and once I'd managed to get across that start line, everything else would be a bonus. I knew I couldn't possibly run the whole way, and the plan was to get as far as possible before the calf muscle gave up. Then I'd see if I could hobble on some more before eventually calling it a day. It was all about how far I could go during the run. At least then I would be a brave little soldier and could say I had given it my best shot. Susan would think I was a hero, would look at me with admiration and love me forever.

The one thing I was determined to be was brave, and I put my hand on my shirt at the spot where I had written "For Mum" in very small letters. "This is for you," I said, as I looked to the skies. This seemed to give me a little more strength as I wondered what she would make of her baby entering a half-marathon. As the youngest of her six children, I was always her baby, even when I reached my 40s. Whenever she introduced me to someone as this, I would usually reply, "Mum, I am 48 and 17 stone, these people have eyesight and not enough imagination to see me as your baby." But underneath the embarrassment I quite liked being Mum's baby, and in that strange moment I felt very close to her, in a way I hadn't done since she had passed away.

Then it was time for the choreographed warm-up, which resembled the biggest aerobics class you could possibly imagine. What it did was to increase the reality that the 10:40am start time was fast approaching. The hairs on the back of my neck were beginning to rise. I genuinely couldn't tell how much of it was nerves and how much of it was excitement. The sense of dread and foreboding had long since departed and now I was really looking forward to the race, which did make me wonder if I had become completely delusional.

As the big screen moved into the final minute, it hit me that it was now going to happen. The crowd counted down the final 30 seconds and I got into the crouched pose that I had witnessed athletes adopt at the start of a long-distance run.

As the counting went into the last five seconds, I braced myself for the off, as I didn't want to get caught by those behind me. I was effectively in the middle of a very large crowd of 'pinkies', and I realised that tripping and becoming a carpet for those following wasn't the start I'd been hoping for. I kept an eye on the runners immediately in front so that I could move at the exact moment they did.

The sound of the gun was amplified through the powerful sound system and my coiled spring was ready to release. But it couldn't do so, as there was no movement from the people in front. After a minute I surfaced from my pose and looked around. The big screens were showing people running across the start line, but there was no movement as far as I could see.

The situation remained the same for the next 20 minutes. The tension began to lift as people chatted amongst themselves to pass the time. It was a surreal situation. We were meant to be in a race, but this was akin to being in the Tesco checkout queue on Christmas Eve. We were still so far from the start line, and there was little sign of progress.

Eventually, we sensed something happening ahead. The crowd started to walk forward in a mass procession similar to the one I'd witnessed when we left the bus, only this one was going a bit slower. We carried on like this for the 20-minutes it took to cover the one-kilometre distance to the start line, finally reaching it 40-minutes after the starter's gun had sounded. This made me realise why we all had those little electronic timing chips tied to our laces.

As we broke into a run just before the line, I made a mental note to add the two-kilometres I had walked to my total distance achieved. Those guys at the front have it way too easy!

We're Off

As I crossed the start line, I found myself jogging along in a sea of people and feeling quite good about things. However, my confidence was lost about 75 yards later, when I saw an 'orange' competitor lying on the pavement being treated by St John Ambulance volunteers. It looked like he was in real agony.

My initial feeling was euphoria. If they followed the Formula 1 approach of ranking DNFs (did not finish) in the order of who got the furthest before retiring, I wasn't going to be last. But then it dawned on me that the poor guy had probably gone over after clipping the kerb in the mad dash from the line. He had no doubt badly hurt himself. I now felt quite guilty about having had that thought. I felt sorry for him, but also strategically positioned myself as far away as possible from the kerbs. I was now right in the centre of the road. This was a lesson I had learnt from years of watching old ladies (and men that drive like them) sitting in the middle lane on the M1.

Four of our group went off at a faster pace and I made no attempt to try and keep up with them. For me, this was all about distance, as time would be irrelevant when I didn't finish. Neil, who remained with me, had a serious knee problem that meant he shouldn't have been doing the race in the first place, just like me. So, us two casualties jogged along together, soaking up the sunshine and the amazing atmosphere, as well as milking the applause from the spectators.

After only 1.5 miles, we suddenly found ourselves running towards the iconic Tyne Bridge and yes, the photo is of me and not the back of a London Bus!

Just when I was beginning to think things couldn't get any better, the Red Arrows flew straight overhead, trailing plumes of red, white and blue. If my jaw had dropped any lower then I probably would have tripped over it.

We crossed the bridge and shortly afterwards met a lady called Ethel, who was to become a real highlight of my day.

As we jogged along, waving back to the crowds, I happened to notice a little elderly lady to my right. She was jogging along but seemed deep in thought and was paying little attention to what was going on around her. She was clearly without anyone to keep her company and so I did the gracious thing and gently steered over in her direction to have a little chat with her as we jogged.

It turned out that Ethel was 83 years old. At this point, I should confess that we weren't in the process of passing her at the time, quite the contrary. If anything, despite Ethel's tiny stature and frail appearance, my money would have been on her if it had come down to a sprint finish. I kept the conversation relatively short as talking and running at the same time isn't easy on your breathing. Unless you are me, that is. As my friends would testify, I could keep talking even if I was drowning.

I left Ethel to concentrate on her running, but after a few minutes I noticed she had started looking from side to side and appeared agitated. At this point, I became concerned. I had this horrible picture of her keeling over and becoming another Great North Run statistic. We then proceeded to have the following conversation:

Me: "Are you ok?"

Ethel: "Yes."

Me: "Are you sure?"

Ethel: "Yes."

Me: "What's wrong?"

Ethel: (Pauses, but continues to look from side to side.) "Nothing."

Me: "Are you looking for someone?"

Ethel: "Yes."

Me: "Are they running?"

Ethel: "No."

Me: "Coming to support you?"

Ethel: "Sort of."

Me: "Sort of?"

Ethel: "My daughter is bringing me my Sunday dinner."

Me: "You are kidding me?"

Ethel: "Nope, I am bloody starving."

Ethel genuinely wasn't pulling my leg. She had actually arranged for her meals-without-wheels to be waiting for her en-route. I tried to negotiate a roast potato if I could locate the meal for her, but Ethel wasn't having any of it. She was a real character and made me feel such an idiot for the fuss I had made about keeping down my breakfast six hours earlier. I would have loved to have had the pleasure of Ethel's company for longer, but she spotted her daughter in the crowd and her dinner was indeed waiting. It really was a Sunday Roast on a china plate with proper cutlery. As she stopped to tuck in, Neil and I waved goodbye and continued on our way with huge smiles on our faces. What a genuinely lovely lady.

We were now leaving Newcastle. This was the first real opportunity I'd had to think about how I felt. The calf muscle wasn't too bad at all and my steady pace meant I wasn't getting too out of breath. So far it was going as well as I could have hoped for, and I started to believe that my eventual retirement could be a respectable one.

I had been so wrapped up in everything going on around me that it was a surprise when I found myself approaching a board with a large Number 5 on it. The realisation set in that I was actually passing the five-mile marker. I had never run further than this before, so if all else failed I was going to record a personal best distance. Whatever happened now, I was definitely going to be pleased with my performance. Just after this, Neil decided that his problems meant he couldn't run any further and he was going to have to walk. I was preparing to do likewise, but he could tell I wanted to see just how far I could get and urged me to continue. From this point I continued running on my own. Well, apart from the several thousand strangers I was with, of course.

It was then I took a left turn onto the A194 and headed in the direction of South Shields.

I was amused by the amount of people I was involved in overtakes with. This was due to the fact they would pass me as they ran at a faster pace than me, and then I would pass them as they got out of breath and had to walk. This cycle was repeated continually with quite a few people. As I continued to chuckle to myself over this game of perpetual leapfrog, it dawned on me that part of the reason for it was that I had been running at a consistent pace and taking regular sips from the bottles of water handed out at three-mile intervals. All in all, I was actually looking after myself quite well, which was surprising considering all of the distractions around me. A variety of bands were playing alongside the course, ranging from rock to country to reggae – another highlight of the day.

The next thing I knew, I was passing the seven-mile marker board. This meant I was now just past the halfway point. I now started to do the one thing that I said I wouldn't do, and that was to raise my expectations. I began to consider that it might actually be possible to run far enough so that when the calf went twang, I could hobble the rest of the way and maybe, just maybe, cross the finish line. I knew I couldn't limp for seven or eight miles, but maybe if I could leave myself three miles or so to limp then finishing just might be possible, even if it was extremely painful. My carefully thought through cautious plan was going quickly out of the window. As I jogged onwards, I continued to dream of crawling over the finish line.

If I'd been having trouble managing my expectations before, this became even worse when I caught sight of the 10-mile marker. I was feeling extremely tired and was beginning to regret not filling up the energy tank, as the anticipated calf-twang was yet to happen. The fuel tank was very low and yet the wheels still hadn't fallen off!

The calf was actually behaving itself better than on any of my previous dozen or so training runs, which had put far less strain on it than this run had. I tried to rationalise the reason for this and even wondered if the dreaded haemorrhoids had caused a beneficial change to my running style. Perhaps I was mincing far more than I realised. I didn't think so, though, as even these little demons had been well behaved. I chose not to worry as to the reason why the run was going so much better than expected and just be grateful that it was.

If my expectations were like a helium balloon gently trying to drift upwards, then this was the moment that the string broke and I completely lost control of all reasoned thought.

I passed that 10-mile marker board and in a moment of complete madness thought to myself, "I can do this, it is only another three miles." To make matters even worse, I looked to the sky and made a promise to my mum that I was going to do it for her. In that one moment, I had put myself in a position where managing to run right to the finish line was the only acceptable result. I had run every step of the first 10 miles, with no stopping or walking, and all I had to do was keep this going for another 3.1 miles. What could possibly go wrong?

The Finish

I am sure most of you have heard of the immortal running phrase “hitting the wall”. Well, I can tell you from experience that this is absolutely not true and you do not hit the wall. The wall actually hits you, and when it does it’s bloody painful!

This is exactly what happened to me only half a mile after the 10-mile marker and the associated commitment I had made to finish the run. My feelings of tiredness were overtaken by a horrible sensation where my muscles felt empty. This is an experience I would never have encountered had I not put myself in this position. It was unlike anything I had experienced before. What happens when the muscles are totally empty is that each movement of the limb is extremely painful. This is the body’s way of telling the brain, “Stop, you dickhead.” Any absence of pain from the calf muscle was more than made up for by an even greater agony. It genuinely felt like hot daggers had been pushed into my thighs.

I had obviously been running on reserve for some time and hadn’t realised there was currently little else to draw on. This wasn’t helped by the fact that I refused to consume any energy drinks or sweets because of my diabetes. With hindsight, I realise that this was, without doubt, my dumbest decision of the day.

Unfortunately, this dickhead wasn't going to stop, partly because of his pig-headed streak but mainly because of the foolish promise he had just made to his mum. If I didn't finish, then I would feel terrible about it for the rest of my life. It was my one chance to shine and I just had to do it.

By now you are probably starting to notice the very significant change in my attitude. The relaxed approach I started out with had now completely disappeared. I was on a mission, and I was desperately hanging on by my fingertips.

The one thing that probably helped is that I had run with pain during my later training runs. However, this was on a different scale entirely. I was clearly in trouble and in some bizarre way this actually worked to my advantage.

On the previous evening, one of my friends had persuaded me to put my name in big letters on the front of my running shirt. I didn't want to do this, as it felt like an act of vanity, but after much persuasion I eventually agreed. It was as I began slowly ascending the long incline up Prince Edward Road towards the South Shields seafront that the reason for me doing this became clear. The crowd of spectators realised I was in a really bad way and their more general cheers and applause were replaced with loud cries of, "Come on, Daryn, you can do it," or variations to that effect. Instead of hearing general applause, the crowd were actually calling to ME. It's impossible to explain just what a huge help this was or the lift it gave me. Somehow this amazing support combined with what limited grit I had left kept me going, as I concentrated on one step at a time. I was still running, albeit not particularly elegantly. The best way I can describe it is if Coco the Clown, complete with his long shoes, had decided to go for a run after 20 pints of Special Brew. I wasn't ready to give in just yet but it was becoming a battle just to stay upright. I knew I had to, as I realised that once I went down I would probably not get up again. I was determined not to give in and the spectators were determined not to let me. The more I struggled, the more support they offered.

I tried to take my mind off the pain and concentrate on what was going on around me. An elderly Mickey and Minnie Mouse were pulling a trolley filled with a bucket full of donations, and they proved a good distraction. I started to engage in jovial banter with the crowd, but humour was becoming as difficult as moving the pain-ridden legs underneath me. Besides, so many of the people leaning on the barriers seemed to have a beer in their hand. I still had my water bottle, but I would have paid virtually anything to swap it for one of those pints. My fixation on the good stuff wasn't helping, so I manoeuvred myself back to the centre of the road to try and concentrate.

One of the things that surprised me about the amazing crowd was how many of them had buckets of sweets, which they held out for the runners to help themselves to. You will recall that if I had not foolishly declined anything sweet throughout the run, I would probably have had a bit more energy in the tank.

Now, as I struggled towards the top of the hill, a lady armed with one of these buckets decided I clearly needed help, which I would surely have agreed with if I hadn't left my brain at the start line. As she saw me approaching, she left the kerb and headed for the centre of the road so that she could ambush me. Now, I don't like to be rude about people, especially when they are being so kind and helpful, but in this case it is relevant to what happened next. Now, I know I'm not exactly anorexic, but this lady was huge, and I do mean huge. Her ankles were actually larger than my thighs and I estimate that she must have been in excess of 30 stone. She obviously found walking very difficult and this made her gesture of bothering to come out to the middle of the road to help me even more admirable.

As she approached me, I could tell she had been dipping into the contents of the bucket, as her cheeks bulged like a chipmunk's after helping itself to a rival's nut store. She must have had at least six boiled sweets in her mouth as she proceeded to do the best impression of Marlon Brando in '*The Godfather*' I have ever seen. She thrust the bucket towards me and, just as I expected Don Vito Corleone to make me an offer I couldn't refuse, she said in her very muffled voice, "Wood yew loik er sweet?"

The correct reply would have been, "Yes, please," but instead I pointed to the large Diabetes UK logo on my running shirt and replied, "No thanks, I have diabetes."

The woman replied, "Yeah, sew doow oi."

This really tickled me, but I feel the irony of her response was totally lost on her.

However, the encounter did help me through the next few minutes, as I couldn't help thinking about the humour of the moment and also the lady's real act of kindness, which I was genuinely moved by.

By the time this wore off, I had reached the top of the hill and faced a relatively short but steep descent. Surprisingly, going down a steep hill was actually more painful than going uphill, as I had to use my now empty thigh muscles to slow myself down and prevent myself from falling flat on my face. This was not as easy as it sounds. Fortunately, it was only about 50 yards down the hill and the presence of an official photographer ensured I didn't whinge too much. It is amazing how in extreme moments such as this one we can still find room for a bit of vanity.

I took a left turn at the bottom of the hill and experienced an enormous mental lift, as I immediately passed the 12-mile marker board and found myself on the seafront. The finish line was now only a mile away, and it was straight ahead of me. To fail now just wasn't worth thinking about. I could feel an adrenalin surge – well, maybe a trickle – within me. I still wasn't overconfident, as I remembered how many times I had seen runners in the London Marathon collapse just yards from the finish line, as all the determination in the world just wouldn't operate their legs. I knew that whilst I had all the mental strength and determination to get me to the line, which admittedly was being severely tested, I couldn't be sure that my body would make it. That last mile seemed to take forever. I kept telling myself to enjoy the moment and the achievement, but I was scared that I (and my dreams) could come crashing down at any moment.

So I got back to taking things one step at a time and watched the boards go by. They first showed 800m to go, then 400m and then 200m. I finally started to believe that I was actually going to make it, even if that involved crawling on all fours. I achieved something else, too, which was picked up by the photographer as I approached the finish line. I had managed to make my face go as pink as the wig that I was wearing.

It must seem quite crazy that after having completed 13 miles and with less than 100 yards to go, I still wasn't 100% convinced I was actually going to make it. I really was struggling so badly that I knew I could collapse at any moment.

And then, suddenly, there was the finish line right in front of me. The feeling I had as I crossed it is one that I will never forget – I was totally and completely knackered!

The normal protocol is to run across the line and then walk to one of the stations to have your timing chip removed. But as I crossed the line two burly stewards spotted the state I was in and rushed to meet me. I didn't understand this at all…until I tried to walk. That is the moment I discovered I no longer had the strength in my legs to support my own weight – it was clearly the momentum of running that had been keeping me upright. Like a couple of prop-forwards in a rugby scrum, they took one arm each. I must confess, this seemed a little over-familiar, but they had obviously seen my kind of pained facial expression and jelly-like legs many times before. As I attempted to stop running and tried to walk, the paralysis kicked in and I genuinely couldn't control my movements from the waist down. This was the first time this had happened to me without alcohol being involved. They helped me away from the finish line so that I didn't get flattened in the stampede, and, yes, there were people who finished after me. Several thousand in fact.

Once I could eventually stand on my own, I thanked my helpers and slowly went to get the chip removed and collect my bag of goodies. I then made my way to the point where I'd previously agreed to meet Susan and my fellow runners. I sat on the grass, mainly because I was too exhausted to stand, and reflected on what had just happened.

I couldn't believe that I had actually completed the whole of the Great North Run from start to finish, without stopping or walking. This was far beyond anything I could have expected at the beginning of the day.

As for the time, I finished it in three hours, 33 minutes and 19 seconds. This could only be described as 'slow', and a paraplegic tortoise comes back to mind, but I didn't care as getting to the finish was all that mattered to me. This Unfit Fat Old bloke with diabetes, an injury, inadequate training and piles had actually done it. I had to keep pinching myself to believe it was true.

I looked up and gave my mum a smug, "I told you I would do it". I said this in a cocky way that portrayed the type of confidence that had been decidedly absent up to this point. I also have to confess there was a little tear in the corner of my eye. I had kept my promise to her and like to think she was really proud of my efforts.

I also thought about that moment, many months earlier, when I'd heard of Tim's death. I proudly repeated the phrase, "I only have diabetes."

Susan arrived and following her initial state of surprise that I had arrived under my own steam, she was genuinely impressed by what I had achieved. She confessed that she had missed me going by, as she had been busy enquiring how the injured would be transported to the finish. I didn't mind her lack of confidence in me, as I'd been the same at the start, but now I was her hero.

I took the opportunity to rest my spent body and replenish it with various energy snacks from the goody bag. Diabetes was definitely not a consideration at this point! When Neil arrived, I was pleased to find out that all of us had completed the distance, as my injured friend had made it to the end after all. Whilst four of the group finished well ahead of me, I was really surprised to discover that I was the only one who ran the whole distance without walking any of it. This made me feel even more proud of my achievement.

I also thought about the fact I had taken part in the run on behalf of Diabetes UK, and had pledged to try and raise £400. In fact, due to the generosity of many people (and selective coercion on my part), the total I'd raised was over £1,200. I had been concerned about taking people's money and not getting very far, but now I felt I really had earned it.

As I sat there in a state of exhaustion that I didn't believe was possible, I was even more surprised when I suddenly blurted out loud, "I want to do this again next year." I really wasn't sure where that came from, and from the look on the others' faces they clearly all thought I was delusional. But I had got such an amazing kick from the whole thing that I thought it might possibly be true.

We decided to go for a well-earned beer and some food and wait for that idiotic feeling to go away. I have to say that I can't recall ever having a better-tasting pint of Guinness.

After a couple of pints, we decided to head back to the cottages in Durham. A couple of us were driving and we weren't sure how long it would be before our legs had stiffened up to the point that we could no longer push the pedals.

Once back, I took a long shower and changed into clothes that were more socially acceptable (I'd had enough of the 'total dick' look for one day). By this time all our muscles were really stiff and we walked around the house as if we were at a Frankenstein convention doing Boris Karloff walk-a-likes!

Unsurprisingly, nobody wanted to drive and we unanimously agreed to attempt to walk to the nearest pub, which was right next door to the cottages. Despite the fact that this involved a walk of only 30 yards at the most, we genuinely considered calling a taxi. But the party of brave little soldiers took on the walking challenge and we managed to make it to the pub without losing anyone along the way. Despite our collective exhaustion, we were all pleased with our efforts and what we had achieved. We had surpassed our expectations and the atmosphere of smugness in the air could have been cut with a chainsaw. This was only interrupted when visits to the bar or the toilet reminded us of our aches and pains. Susan was a great help with the visits to the bar, but not much help with the loo trips.

By the time we came to leave and make our way back to the cottages, our legs had fully succumbed and the Boris Karloff impressions were now more reminiscent of the Tin Man from '*The Wizard of Oz*' (before the oil was applied). It was genuinely so bad that I wasn't the only one who had to stop for a break on the 30-yard journey home. But we dug deep and got through the front door before literally climbing the stairs and turning in for a good night's sleep.

Just before closing my eyes, I not only reflected on what I had just achieved, but also the fact that neither my calf muscle nor the haemorrhoids had given me any trouble. I certainly couldn't complain, as fate had certainly smiled on me. I don't recall if I had any dreams that night, but I am confident that if I did then they would have been good ones. In all honesty, I suspect I was too knackered even to dream.

After a good rest and some breakfast, we headed off back to Essex. I was driving and didn't really have much trouble due to three factors: dual carriageway all the way, an automatic car and cruise control. This meant I could rest the lead pipes below the waist until we reached home.

It had been an amazing weekend, and one that I will never forget.

And Then...

I have to say that this should have been the end of the story, as there should have been absolutely no point in writing another chapter. This was intended to be a one-off and that was now over. The End!

The trouble is, when I crossed the finish line I had this idiotic feeling that I wanted to do it all again. I waited three months for this feeling to subside, but it didn't. I am quite confident that it would have done had it not been for two things. Firstly, I received a letter from the organisers of the Great North Run saying that as I had finished the race, I qualified for automatic entry for the next three years and wouldn't have to enter the ballot. Unfortunately, this still involved paying the entry fee but the 'automatic entry' was pouring paraffin on the flames of the urge I was trying to put out.

The final straw came when I had dinner with my good friends Lorraine and Paul, whom I have known since we did our apprenticeships together. I happened to mention that I was having this ridiculous urge to do the Great North Run again. This is the point where I could rely on Paul to wet himself with laughter and pour total ridicule on any thoughts of me doing something that involved exercise other than lifting a pint. I could rely on Paul to extinguish my urge quicker than a troop of boy scouts with full bladders could put out a campfire. Well, this was the plan, but instead of the anticipated mockery, Paul calmly responded with the words, "I will do it with you." Once I realised he was actually being serious, my fate was sealed.

I think it's safe to say that Paul's situation at that time was not a million miles away from where I had started nine months previously. He was a year younger than me, carried a few (!) extra pounds and his general fitness was also far from what you would call athletic. In short, he was nearly as old, nearly as fat and nearly as unfit as I had been. The only real difference was that he had not succumbed to diabetes, despite trying very hard. Although he has never stated this, I am convinced he had thought to himself, "If that fat old bugger can do it, then I'm sure I can." Oh, how I love to inspire people.

So, true to his word, Paul put in his application for the 2010 Great North Run. Unfortunately, he didn't get picked out in the main ballot but he did secure a charity place on behalf of Prostate Cancer UK. He decided on the charity because my eldest brother, Michael, had only just recovered from this type of cancer. My family and I were very grateful to Paul for making this choice.

Paul and I go back a very long way and we can read each other like a book. I knew he was taking the race seriously and consequently took up my automatic place. It was game on.

Back Again?

We set about training for the big event. As far as the preparation was concerned, it all went extremely well, which meant it didn't provide so many humorous anecdotes. This may have been good for the run, but it wasn't much help for this book!

This time there was a lot in my favour. I had eight months to train instead of four, my weight was lower – although I was still far from anorexic – and I was starting from a better fitness level. I wasn't exactly the stereotypical image of an athlete, but I liked to think that instead of being a UFO, I was merely a ufo. To be precise, I guess it should be ufO, as I certainly hadn't improved my age in the last year, other than in the way you would describe a fine wine. Others may think comparing me to wine is more like, "Full bodied and does your head in!"

A carefully managed training programme that involved gradually increasing my distance worked well. The calf muscle was still a concern, as I found it flared up if I tried to push it too hard, but I learnt that doing an extensive warm up and staying at a comfortable pace on each training run helped me avoid any significant problems. It wasn't long before I found myself managing six-mile runs through Thetford Forest without too much trouble. Paul and I entered a few 10km fun runs to give us something to work for and by the time we got to September we were both in quite good shape (for us).

So, when it came to the big weekend, Lorraine, Paul, Susan and I headed off for the North East and the caravan we had booked just north of Newcastle. The weekend went similarly to the previous year, apart from – I am pleased to say – the haemorrhoids. Lorraine and Susan adopted supporting roles, which mainly involved drinking the alcohol that we were not allowed to consume prior to the race.

My attitude this time around was quite different. I was calm, relaxed and really looking forward to it. I still felt anxious, as I couldn't be sure if I would go through the same pain as last time, but I was confident that it couldn't be any worse.

On the other hand, Paul was showing the signs of nerves and anxiety that I had experienced the year before. This is not surprising, as it really is the fear of the unknown that is the most difficult to deal with. I knew what was coming and that I was far better prepared for it than I had been 12-months previously. All Paul had to rely on was the knowledge that if the fat old bloke he had known for so long could do it then surely he could too.

Humour can be a good way of reducing the tension in these situations, so I set about my usual style of constant wisecracking. I'm never sure if this style helps or is just plain irritating, but this dilemma has never stopped me in the past, so there was no reason to be any different this time.

One of the things I haven't mentioned is how many of the 'pinkies' at the back of the start formation were in fancy dress this time around. They ranged from a pantomime horse to a giant beer bottle, and just about everything in between. They were a great source of distraction and Paul and I were impressed and amused by the level of effort that everyone had obviously put into the costumes.

The seven ladies immediately in front of us were all dressed up in Wonder Woman costumes. Now, not wishing to be completely sexist, a Wonder Woman costume is a pleasant view from any angle, including the rear. For those of you who are too young to remember, do a Google search for Linda Carter in the TV series. You will understand exactly what I mean.

Of course, the presence of the women provided the perfect opportunity for mirth to distract Paul with. Well, that is my excuse and I am definitely sticking to it. When the race started we found ourselves jogging along behind the ladies, which was not the most unpleasant part of the day. We joked about having a favourite Wonder Woman and I found myself drawn to one in particular. However, despite my good intention of trying to distract Paul, my laddish behaviour was to get the outcome it deserved.

After about a mile, the Wonder Women began to drop their pace and Paul and I decided we needed to pass them. We had agreed beforehand the pace that we wanted to run and I was able to monitor our performance on the clever running watch I had bought the year before. Whilst this may sound completely unnecessary, it is really easy to find yourself running at someone else's pace, especially when you are in a large group of runners.

So, as the Wonder Women slowed we moved to the side and slowly passed them. I couldn't resist turning my head and giving my 'favourite' a little smile. What I didn't expect was for HIM to smile back. Yes, this Wonder Woman had a full beard and almost certainly other attributes that differentiated him from the other Wonder Women. This was a group of six ladies and one man. They were all dressed in the same costume, and I had been admiring the arse of the bloke! Paul laughed so much that I thought he was going to choke. He couldn't stop smiling for quite some time and clearly enjoyed my embarrassment and discomfort, which I do confess was well deserved.

As for the rest of the race, it couldn't have been more different to the previous year. Paul and I managed a good, steady pace throughout. Apparently, I talked the whole way round, leading Paul to refer to me as his personal iPod, but "without the ability to switch the bloody thing off!"

We felt so good that we were able to up the pace for the last mile and we finished with not far off a serious sprint. I finished the race in two hours and 47 minutes – a 46-minute improvement on the previous year.

Paul and I returned to Newcastle to complete the run in 2011, finishing in two hours and 36 minutes, and we went back again in 2012, finishing in two hours and 43 minutes. The latter time wasn't so good, as I'd suffered a bad stomach virus on holiday just four weeks before the run. I could explain more, but trust me, you really wouldn't want me to. When Paul asked where my pace and stamina had gone, I replied, "I left it in a gite in France."

So, looking back on 'the journey', it certainly hadn't been what I had expected. I didn't think I would end up completing the Great North Run four times without ever stopping to walk. I would be the first to accept that the times weren't fantastic, but I don't really care as it was never about my speed. I don't think anyone worries about the time it took them to climb Mount Everest, as getting to the pinnacle is the only thing that counts. Running the whole distance of the Great North Run was my pinnacle, and I managed it more than once.

Afterword

On Reflection

Writing this book has been a great reminder of how it all began – with my big mouth and ego getting me into a pickle. It's definitely not the first time this has happened in my life. The initial objective was just to survive and not become another Great North Run statistic. Of course, the other objective was to not lose face in front of Susan, and I think I managed to achieve both. I am still alive and we now live together in Cornwall. But I have to say that there are far easier ways of impressing your new girlfriend.

What I never expected was to discover that I am actually capable of achieving more than I ever used to think. All it took was determination, a lot of practice, willingness to push past my perceived limits and, of course, a various assortment of medicinal creams.

The one thing that did come as a complete surprise was the sense of achievement I feel and the significant improvement to my self-esteem. Like most people, getting older had been causing me some angst, but now I can feel really proud of myself. I don't need to prove anything to anyone else. Most importantly, I don't need to prove anything to myself.

The four medals hang proudly on my office wall and

the commemorative t-shirts from each year hang in my wardrobe. Every time they catch my eye, it reminds me of what I achieved and what we are capable of.

I will continue the journey through middle age with my head held high.

About the Author

Daryn lives with his partner, Susan, in Cornwall, having emigrated from East Anglia, where he spent most of his life. He has three grown-up daughters and four grandchildren. Well, this is so far – he isn't convinced they are done with breeding just yet.

For his day job he runs a business consultancy and will continue to do so until this book becomes a bestseller. As this is his first book, it will certainly become HIS bestseller, which may not be enough to convince the mortgage company of his sudden career change.

Through his business work, Daryn is also involved in public speaking, and more recently became a speaker for Diabetes UK. His serious talks about the condition led to lighter, more humorous ones about his own journey with type 2 diabetes, which he delivers at fundraising events for good causes. He decided to put his story in writing after being spurred on by the positive feedback he's received following these speaking engagements.